# WE THE PEOPLE

# Great Women of the Civil War

## by Lucia Raatma

Content Adviser: Lisa Laskin, Ph.D.,
Department of History,
Harvard University

Reading Adviser: Susan Kesselring, M.A.,
Literacy Educator,
Rosemount-Apple Valley-Eagan (Minnesota) School District

**COMPASS POINT BOOKS**
**MINNEAPOLIS, MINNESOTA**

Compass Point Books
151 Good Counsel Drive
P.O. Box 669
Mankato, MN 56002-0669
877-845-8392
www.capstonepub.com

On the cover: Harriet Beecher Stowe, author of *Uncle Tom's Cabin*,
with a group of fellow antislavery workers

Photographs ©: Hulton/Archive by Getty Images, cover, 16; Prints Old & Rare, back cover (far
left); Library of Congress, back cover, 5, 8, 10, 12, 20, 21, 26, 29, 34, 40; Nancy Carter/North
Wind Picture Archives, 4; Corbis, 6, 27, 38; North Wind Picture Archives, 9, 11, 25;
DVIC/NARA, 13; The Newberry Library/Stock Montage, 14; Bettmann/Corbis, 15, 24; Michigan
State Archives, 17; MPI/Getty Images, 18, 41; National Park Service, 30; AP/Wide World
Photos/General Services Administration, 31; AP/Wide World Photos/The Daily Leader/Thomas
Wells, 32; Disderi & Co./Hulton/Archive by Getty Images, 33; Documenting the American South,
The University of North Carolina at Chapel Hill, 36; Courtesy of Manuscripts and Rare Books
Department, Earl Gregg Swem Library, College of William and Mary, 37.

Creative Director: Terri Foley
Managing Editor: Catherine Neitge
Editor: Nadia Higgins
Photo Researcher: Svetlana Zhurkina
Designer/Page production: Bradfordesign, Inc./Bobbie Nuytten
Cartographer: XNR Productions, Inc.
Educational Consultant: Diane Smolinski

**Library of Congress Cataloging-in-Publication Data**
Raatma, Lucia.
  Great women of the Civil War / by Lucia Raatma.
    p. cm—(We the people)
  Includes bibliographical references (p.   ) and index.
  ISBN-13: 978-0-7565-0839-5 (hardcover)  ISBN-10: 0-7565-0839-8 (hardcover)
  ISBN-13: 978-0-7565-1770-0 (paperback)  ISBN-10: 0-7565-1770-2 (paperback)
  1. United States—History—Civil War, 1861-1865—Women—Juvenile literature. 2.
Women—United States—History—19th century—Juvenile literature. 3. Women—United
States—Biography—Juvenile literature. I. Title. II. We the people (Series) (Compass Point
Books)
  E628.R225 2004
  973.7'082—dc22                          2004016301

Printed in the United States of America in Stevens Point, Wisconsin.  032011     006103R

# TABLE OF CONTENTS

# WAR BETWEEN THE STATES

When you think of war, you probably think of two or more nations fighting one another. However, the American Civil War was not a conflict between the United States and another country. Instead, it was a war *within* the United States, with Northern and Southern states in battle against each other. Considering that the war was fought in the mid-1800s, you also probably picture all the soldiers as men. While men did most

*Modern actors re-create life at a Civil War army camp.*

4

of the fighting, women did not sit back and watch. They stepped forward and took important and sometimes surprising roles during the war.

The Civil War came about because some Southern states decided to leave, or secede, from the United States. They wanted to form a separate country, but the North strongly opposed them.

*One woman poses with a group of men at an army post office in Virginia, around 1862.*

The main issue that divided North and South was slavery. Before the Civil War began, slavery was legal in the Southern states but illegal in most of the Northern states. In the South, farming was the main way to make money, and much of the farmwork was done by slaves. These slaves' ancestors had been taken from their homes in Africa and brought to the United States against their will. The black slaves were bought and sold like livestock. Many were terribly mistreated by their owners.

6

*Black slaves work on a cotton plantation in the South before the Civil War.*

By the mid-1800s, many people in the North were strongly opposed to slavery. The Southern states feared that the government would put an end to the practice. In December 1860, South Carolina became the first Southern state to secede from the United States. During the next six months, 10 more Southern states seceded. Together they formed the Confederate States of America, also known as the Confederacy. The North remained the United States of America and was also known as the Union.

*This map shows Union and Confederate states, as well as major battles of the Civil War.*

**7**

The Confederacy and the Union were at war for four years, from April 1861 to May 1865. At times, families were torn apart, with some members agreeing with the Union while others sided with the Confederacy. Some say the war was one of brother against brother, and that was often the case.

*Union soldiers (in blue uniforms) and Confederate soldiers (in gray uniforms) battle each other at Winchester, Virginia. More Americans died in the Civil War than in any other war in history.*

8

*A group of women cheers on Union troops as the soldiers march to war.*

As these men faced one another on battlefields each day, women found their roles changing. In the 1860s, women were expected to become wives and mothers. Very few had professional careers, since education was usually not considered important for women.

When the Civil War began, however, nearly every family was affected in some way, as husbands and

9

*This magazine cover from 1861 shows women making weapons for Union troops (top image). The women are doing work similar to that of the men below.*

brothers left home to become soldiers. While the men were away, some women had to take jobs that were previously considered "men's work."

Women served as clerks and factory workers. They worked the family farms or continued to keep a family business operating. Many women volunteered as nurses, organized small hospitals, rolled bandages, and gathered supplies for the troops. Some led the fight against slavery.

In addition to all these women who worked away

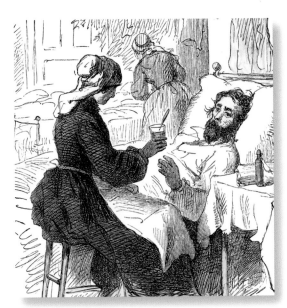

*A female nurse treats a wounded soldier at an army hospital. Before the Civil War, most nurses were men.*

from the battlefields, there were a number of women who played key roles in battles. Some gave medical care to wounded soldiers, while others acted as spies. On rare occasions, some women even traveled with their husbands into combat.

11

*This woman, perhaps a soldier's wife, appears to be doing laundry for troops stationed at an army camp in Washington, D.C.*

A handful of these women are now famous, while others are not so well known. All these women proved that the Civil War touched every American, and their actions had a long-lasting effect.

12

# HARRIET BEECHER STOWE

One of the most recognized names from Civil War times is Harriet Beecher Stowe. She was a white woman born in Connecticut, a free state in the North. Stowe grew up hearing antislavery sermons that her father, a minister, would often preach. Her mother encouraged her to read and learn as much as she could. Stowe married and had seven children. In addition to being a wife and mother, she was a gifted writer. In 1852, nine years before the Civil War began, she published a book called

*Harriet Beecher Stowe at around age 65*

**13**

# UNCLE TOM'S CABIN;

OR,

# LIFE AMONG THE LOWLY.

BY

HARRIET BEECHER STOWE.

VOL. II.

BOSTON:
JOHN P. JEWETT & COMPANY.
CLEVELAND, OHIO:
JEWETT, PROCTOR & WORTHINGTON.
1852.

*The title page from an 1852 edition of* Uncle Tom's Cabin

*Uncle Tom's Cabin.* This book told the story of a slave named Uncle Tom who suffers at the hands of a harsh master named Simon Legree.

135,000 SETS, 270,000 VOLUMES SOLD.

# UNCLE TOM'S CABIN

## FOR SALE HERE.

AN EDITION FOR THE MILLION, COMPLETE IN 1 Vol., PRICE 37 1-2 CENTS.
"      "      IN GERMAN, IN 1 Vol., PRICE 50 CENTS.
"      "      IN 2 Vols., CLOTH, 6 PLATES, PRICE $1.50.
SUPERB ILLUSTRATED EDITION, IN 1 Vol., WITH 153 ENGRAVINGS,
PRICES FROM $2.50 TO $5.00.

## The Greatest Book of the Age.

*A poster advertising* Uncle Tom's Cabin

*Uncle Tom's Cabin* sold more than 300,000 copies—a huge number for the 1800s—and was read by people throughout the world. The book brought attention to the subject of slavery. It was praised by many, while others—especially slave owners in the South—were critical of Stowe for writing such a story.

Some people believe that the publication of *Uncle Tom's Cabin* led to the Civil War because it forced people to really look at the issue of slavery. Most people knew that slavery existed, but many did not realize how unfair and violent it could be. When President Abraham Lincoln was introduced to Stowe in 1862, it is said that he replied, "So you are the little lady who wrote the book that started this great war."

Whether she meant to start a war or not, Stowe did stir up a lot of disagreements with her writing. She wrote a column for a newspaper called *The Independent*, in which she urged men and women throughout the United States to oppose slavery.

*Harriet Beecher Stowe (front row, third from left) with a group of female abolitionists*

# SOJOURNER TRUTH

Another strong voice in the fight against slavery was Sojourner Truth. Around the year 1797, she was born as a slave named Isabella Baumfree in New York. She had a number of owners until 1828, when New York outlawed slavery. Later, she moved to New York City and made a living as a housekeeper.

In 1843, she had a powerful religious experience. She felt that God had spoken to her and given her a new mission in life. She changed her name to Sojourner Truth—a name she said God gave to her. The word *sojourner* means a person who travels. She devoted the rest of her life to traveling the country and preaching the truth.

*This poster announces an upcoming talk by Sojourner Truth.*

**17**

One year later, she heard speeches by Frederick Douglass and William Lloyd Garrison. These famous men were abolitionists, people who fought to end slavery. She became even more passionate about working for fairness and equality among people.

Sojourner Truth spoke out for the rights of women and slaves and anyone she felt was being mistreated. At

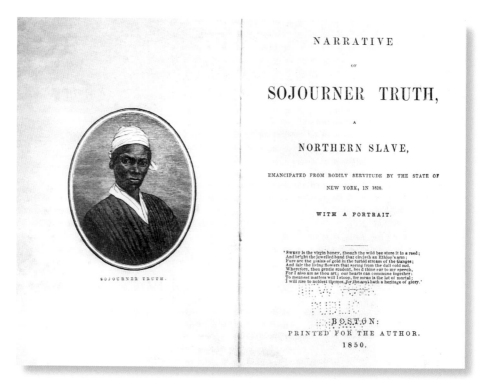

*The title page of an 1850 edition of Sojourner Truth's autobiography*

6 feet (1.8 meters) tall, she had a powerful presence. She gave public speeches, and she was a wonderful singer. Though she couldn't read or write, she told her life story to a writer, and in 1850 her autobiography, *Narrative of Sojourner Truth*, was published.

During the Civil War, she traveled to Washington, D.C., and fought for the desegregation of public transportation in that city. In those days, blacks and whites were segregated, or separated, in many places. Sojourner Truth thought that blacks and whites should be able to sit side by side. The story goes that she once stopped traffic in Washington when a streetcar driver refused to let her board an all-white car. She stood her ground, gained the support of the crowd, and finally was allowed in the car. While in Washington, she also met with President Lincoln at the White House.

After the war, Sojourner Truth focused her efforts on helping newly freed slaves. She also led a

*Sojourner Truth visited President Abraham Lincoln at the White House in Washington, D.C., in 1864. Lincoln is showing her a Bible that had been given to him by African-Americans in Baltimore, Maryland.*

movement to provide land in Kansas to former slaves and worked with the woman suffrage movement. In the 1800s, women in the United States were not allowed to vote, and she saw this as yet another unfair practice to fight.

# HARRIET TUBMAN

While Harriet Beecher Stowe and Sojourner Truth fought slavery with their words, a woman named Harriet Tubman was taking action. She was born as a slave named Araminta Ross in Maryland around 1820. Over the years, she was harshly punished by her master and saw other slaves whipped and mistreated as well.

She also suffered a serious head injury when she tried to help another slave who was about to be beaten. The supervisor was so angry with her for interfering that he fractured her skull with a heavy weight. She was unconscious for a number of days, and she experienced blackouts on and off for the rest of her life.

*Harriet Tubman at around age 45*

In 1844, she married John Tubman. She took his last name and also decided to take her mother's first name of Harriet. Five years later, she heard that she and the other slaves on her plantation were about to be sold. She knew it was time to run away. Her husband did not want to go with her, so she planned her escape with her two brothers instead.

They crept off the plantation one night and began following the North Star, a bright light in the dark sky. At one point, her brothers turned back, but Tubman continued on. She knew that dogs might be chasing her. She also knew she would be beaten if she were caught, but she tried not to be afraid. To her, gaining freedom was worth all of the risk. She followed the star north and finally made it to Philadelphia, Pennsylvania. There she got work as a housekeeper.

After gaining her freedom, Tubman could have stopped, but her own freedom was not enough. She wanted to help others escape slavery, too. During the 1850s, she worked on the Underground Railroad guiding slaves to freedom. The Underground Railroad was not actually a railroad. It was a network of safe places where escaped slaves could stop and rest as they traveled north.

*This map shows the Underground Railroad routes that slaves took from different areas.*

**23**

Through her own experiences of traveling north, Tubman knew the land well. She went back to Southern slave-holding states 18 times and helped around 300 people, including her elderly parents, find freedom. Her work was dangerous, though. Every time she went south, she risked being captured again. Slave owners knew her and put a bounty on her head. They were willing to pay lots of money for Tubman to be captured.

24    *Runaway slaves are welcomed at a stop along the Underground Railroad in the 1850s.*

*An escaped slave is captured by armed men.*

Yet she never gave in. She risked her life and her freedom over and over again, so others could have better lives. Tubman also refused to be stopped by those who lost their courage and put the lives of the others in the group in danger. If anyone she was helping suddenly decided to turn back, she was known to have pulled out a gun and said, "You'll be free or die a slave!"

*Harriet Tubman at 91, two years before she died*

During the Civil War, Harriet Tubman sometimes served as a spy as well. She organized a group of former slaves and had them keep an eye on Confederate troops. They reported to her, and she passed the information along to Union military leaders. Her work as a spy led to the release of hundreds of slaves.

Tubman became known as the Moses of Her People, because her efforts were like those of Moses. In the Bible, Moses helps free slaves called Israelites. The words on her grave read "Servant of God, Well Done."

# CLARA BARTON

Today, many women are nurses, but before the Civil War, nursing was primarily a job for men. Clara Barton, however, found her calling on the battlefield helping wounded men by bringing supplies and acting as a nurse. She earned the nickname Angel of the Battlefield.

Barton was born in 1821 in Massachusetts. Though she was terribly shy as a child, she was very curious and enjoyed the outdoors. As she grew older, she became a teacher and—overcoming her shyness—took pride in sharing her knowledge with children. She was committed to improving children's lives, and for a time, she even taught without pay.

*Clara Barton at around age 44*

In 1854, Barton lost her teaching job to a man simply because she was a woman. She then moved to Washington, D.C., where she served as the first female clerk in the U.S. Patent Office, a division that grants legal rights to inventors.

After the war broke out in 1861, Barton saw that the Army Medical Department was not prepared to care for all the wounded soldiers. When she heard that the 6th Massachusetts Regiment had lost its supplies in battle, she tried to help. She tore up old bed sheets to use as towels, and she cooked for the troops. As the war continued, she heard of more supply shortages. So she worked with Senator Henry Wilson of Massachusetts and advertised in newspapers about the soldiers' needs. People sent in huge amounts of supplies, and Barton then delivered these supplies to the battlefield.

She comforted the men who were hurt, made food for them, and brought them water. As bullets flew all around her, Barton must have been frightened, but she never showed it. She once got typhoid fever, a dangerous disease, but she refused to stop working.

In 1862, Barton tended to soldiers during some of the worst battles of the war, including the battle of Antietam, Maryland, and the Virginia battles of Cedar Mountain, Second Bull Run, and Fredericksburg.

*Clara Barton aided soldiers during the battle of Antietam on September 17, 1862. During this one day, 23,000 men were killed, wounded, or went missing.*

By 1863, the Army Medical Department was better prepared to help the wounded, but no one forgot the remarkable efforts of Clara Barton. By June 1864, she was superintendent of nurses under Union Major General Benjamin F. Butler.

*This memorial to Clara Barton stands at the Antietam National Battlefield in Maryland.*

*This sign was posted in Clara Barton's office in Washington, D.C., after the war.*

As the war ended, Clara Barton began a campaign to help find soldiers who were missing. She published lists in newspapers and wrote letters to families. This work left her exhausted, so in 1869 she went to Europe for a rest. Once there, Barton became involved with a war between France and Prussia (a country that is now part of Germany). She worked with a new organization called the Red Cross to help French citizens affected by the war. This work had a great influence on her.

After she returned to the United States in 1873, she established the American Red Cross, a group that today helps victims of wars and natural disasters, such as fires, earthquakes, and floods. Barton once said, "You must never so much as think whether you like it or not, whether it is bearable or not; you must never think of anything except the need, and how to meet it."

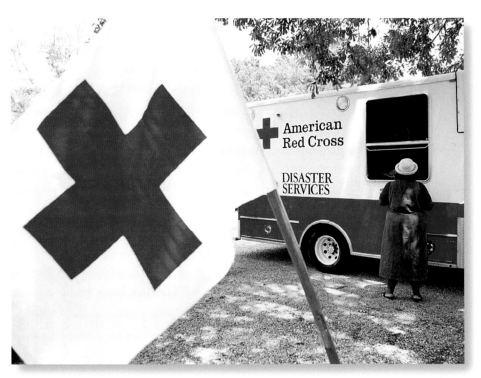

*Today, the American Red Cross is one of the largest charities in the United States. Its white flag with a red cross in the center is known to millions of people.*

## SECRET SPIES

Today when you think of spies, you might imagine James Bond or another character with a lot of special training and high-tech equipment. In the Civil War, though, spies were often not specially trained. A spy could be a society lady or a slave. Spies couldn't pass messages by using e-mail or telephones, either. They often carried secret messages under their big hoop skirts instead!

One such spy was Rose O'Neal Greenhow. She was born in 1817 in Maryland and, as an adult, became a well-known figure in Washington, D.C.,

*Female spies hid secret messages in their big skirts. Sometimes they stuffed messages inside their buns of hair, such as the one shown here.*

**33**

society. She fully supported the Confederacy and began secretly helping the Southern states. It is said that she sent a message to Confederate General Pierre G.T. Beauregard—one so valuable that he was able to win the first battle of Bull Run in 1861.

*Rose O'Neal Greenhow with her daughter*

When the Union discovered what she had been doing, Greenhow was forced to keep to her home in Washington. Even then, with the help of other women, she managed to pass along messages to the Confederacy. It is said that some of her mysterious messages were carried in such places as a woman's bun of hair.

Later, Greenhow was told to leave Washington, D.C., and was sent to live in the Confederate states. Confederate President Jefferson Davis welcomed her warmly, but her story doesn't end here.

At Davis's request, Greenhow went to Great Britain and France, where she spoke out in support of the Confederacy. She published a book called *My Imprisonment* about her experiences in the war. She also met with government leaders in both London and Paris.

On the way home in 1864, her ship, the *Condor*, was chased by a Union ship and ran aground on a sandbar near Cape Fear in Wilmington, North Carolina. She tried to escape to shore in a rowboat. Her boat turned over,

MY IMPRISONMENT

AND THE

FIRST YEAR OF ABOLITION RULE
AT WASHINGTON.

BY

MRS. GREENHOW.

LONDON:
RICHARD BENTLEY,
PUBLISHER IN ORDINARY TO HER MAJESTY.
1863.

*The title page from Rose O'Neal Greenhow's book,* My Imprisonment

though, and she drowned. Some say that she was dragged down by the gold she was carrying, money she had received for the sale of her book.

Hailed as a Confederate hero, Greenhow had a military funeral. Her coffin was wrapped in the Confederate flag, and she was buried in the Oakdale Cemetery in Wilmington, Delaware.

On the other side of the war were Mary Elizabeth Bowser and Elizabeth Van Lew. Bowser was born near Richmond, Virginia, and was a slave for much of her life in the Van Lew household. Upon the death of her father in 1851, Elizabeth Van Lew freed all the slaves he had owned and sent Bowser to Philadelphia, Pennsylvania, to attend school.

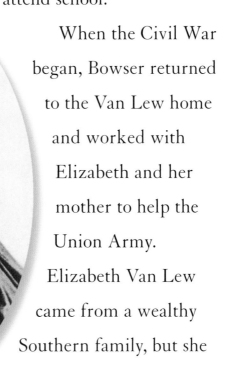

*Elizabeth Van Lew*

When the Civil War began, Bowser returned to the Van Lew home and worked with Elizabeth and her mother to help the Union Army. Elizabeth Van Lew came from a wealthy Southern family, but she did not agree with the practice of slavery. She

**37**

*The Van Lew family mansion in Richmond, Virginia, was run
by slaves until Elizabeth freed them all in 1851.*

38

was so outspoken about her support of the North that some of her neighbors called her Crazy Bet. They thought that only a crazy person could live in Richmond, the capital of the Confederacy, and yet side with the Union.

Van Lew had a number of servants working for her as spies. She got Bowser a job at the Confederate White House. There, Bowser pretended to be uneducated, but all the while she listened to everything that Jefferson Davis, the Confederate president, said. Davis and the leaders he met with thought that Bowser was a slave, so they freely spoke in front of her.

Mary Elizabeth Bowser had a remarkable memory and recited word for word the war plans she had overheard. Then Bowser reported all that she heard to Elizabeth Van Lew, who passed the information along to Union leaders. Bowser also sent information through ordinary, everyday tasks. Once, while putting laundry out to dry on a clothesline, she hung a white shirt

*Jefferson Davis (seated, third from left) and his advisers were tricked by Mary Elizabeth Bowser.*

beside an upside-down pair of pants. That meant, "General Hill is moving troops to the west." Today, Mary Elizabeth Bowser is not a well-known name, but she was a brave woman who took risks to help the Union Army.

No matter what side they were loyal to, the women of the Civil War wanted to do their part.

Whether they quietly worked in hospitals or bravely helped slaves to escape, they were not satisfied to sit back and wait for the war to end. They voiced their opinions, used their clever minds, and did all they could to make a difference.

*Women work at a Union hospital during the Civil War.*

**41**

# GLOSSARY

**abolitionists**—people who fought to end slavery

**autobiography**—a nonfiction book about the author's own life story

**bounty**—a reward offered for the capture of a criminal

**plantation**—a large farm in the South that usually used slave labor to grow one main cash crop such as tobacco, cotton, or rice

**sandbar**—a ridge of sand that sticks up from the bottom of the ocean, especially along the coast

**segregated**—separated by race

**streetcar**—a buslike vehicle that travels on rails like a train

**suffrage**—the right to vote

# DID YOU KNOW?

- In 1978 and 1995, the U.S. government honored Harriet Tubman by issuing postage stamps with her name and image on them. Clara Barton received the same honor in 1948 and 1995, as did Sojourner Truth in 1986.

- Author Mark Twain lived next door to Harriet Beecher Stowe while she lived in Hartford, Connecticut. He wrote famous books such as *The Adventures of Tom Sawyer* and *Huckleberry Finn*.

- During her 18 missions on the Underground Railroad, Harriet Tubman was almost captured on a number of occasions. One close call came about in Maryland after Tubman had just bought some live chickens. Tubman spotted her former owner walking nearby. Thinking quickly, she released the chickens and chased after them. In all the confusion, her old owner didn't have a chance to recognize her, and she got away.

- In 1995, Mary Elizabeth Bowser was inducted into the U.S. Army Intelligence Hall of Fame.

# IMPORTANT DATES

## Timeline

| | |
|---|---|
| **1849** | Harriet Tubman escapes from slavery. |
| **1852** | Harriet Beecher Stowe publishes *Uncle Tom's Cabin*. |
| **1861** | On April 12, the Civil War begins. |
| **1862** | Clara Barton begins working as a nurse on the battlefield. |
| **1864** | Sojourner Truth meets with President Lincoln in Washington, D.C.; Rose O'Neal Greenhow drowns on her way back from Europe. |
| **1865** | On April 9, Confederate General Robert E. Lee surrenders; the Civil War ends in May. |
| **1881** | The American Red Cross is founded by Clara Barton. |

# IMPORTANT PEOPLE

## CLARA BARTON (1821-1912)
*Civil War nurse who went on to found the American Red Cross*

## MARY ELIZABETH BOWSER (1839-?)
*Former slave who spied on Jefferson Davis and gave information to the Union forces*

## ROSE O'NEAL GREENHOW (1817-1864)
*Washington, D.C., woman who spied on the Union and gave information to the Confederacy*

## HARRIET BEECHER STOWE (1811-1896)
*Author of* Uncle Tom's Cabin, *a book that portrayed the cruelty of slavery*

## SOJOURNER TRUTH (1797?-1883)
*Former slave who fought for equal rights for African-Americans and women*

## HARRIET TUBMAN (1820?-1913)
*Woman who escaped slavery and then helped others escape slavery through the Underground Railroad*

## ELIZABETH VAN LEW (1818-1900)
*Southern woman who organized a group of spies working for the Union*

# WANT TO KNOW MORE?

## At the Library

Ford, Carin T. *Daring Women of the Civil War.* Berkeley Heights, N.J.:
Enslow, 2004.

Lutz, Norma Jean. *Sojourner Truth: Abolitionist, Suffragist, Preacher.*
Philadelphia: Chelsea House, 2000.

Ransom, Candice F. *Clara Barton.* Minneapolis: Lerner, 2003.

Sullivan, George. *Harriet Tubman.* New York: Scholastic Reference, 2002.

## On the Web

For more information on this topic, use FactHound.

1. Go to *www.facthound.com*

2. Type in this book ID: 0756508398

3. Click on the *Fetch It* button.

FactHound will find the best Web sites for you.

## On the Road

**Harriet Beecher Stowe Center**
77 Forest St.
Hartford, CT 06105
860/522-9258
To visit Harriet Beecher Stowe's
home and library

**The Harriet Tubman Home**
180 South St.
Auburn, NY 13201
315/252-2081
To tour the home of the "Moses of
Her People"

**Look for more We the People books about this era:**

*The Assassination of Abraham Lincoln*

*The Battle of Gettysburg*

*The Carpetbaggers*

*The Emancipation Proclamation*

*The Underground Railroad*

A complete list of We the People titles is available on our Web site:
www.compasspointbooks.com

# INDEX

## About the Author

Lucia Raatma received her bachelor's degree in English literature from the University of South Carolina and her master's degree in cinema studies from New York University. She has written a wide range of books for young people. When she is not researching or writing, she enjoys going to movies, practicing yoga, and spending time with her family. She lives in New York.